CONTENTS

Words in **bold** are explained in the glossary on page 31.

Page 4   What is a Material?

Page 5   Properties of Materials

Page 6   Wood

Page 10   Plastic

Page 14   Metal

Page 18   Glass

Page 22   Rock

Page 26   Water

Page 30   Fun Facts

Page 31   Glossary

Page 32   Index

WHAT IS A MATERIAL?

Materials are the **substances** from which things are made. There are 300,000 different known materials and this number is still increasing. We use a wide range of different materials every single day.

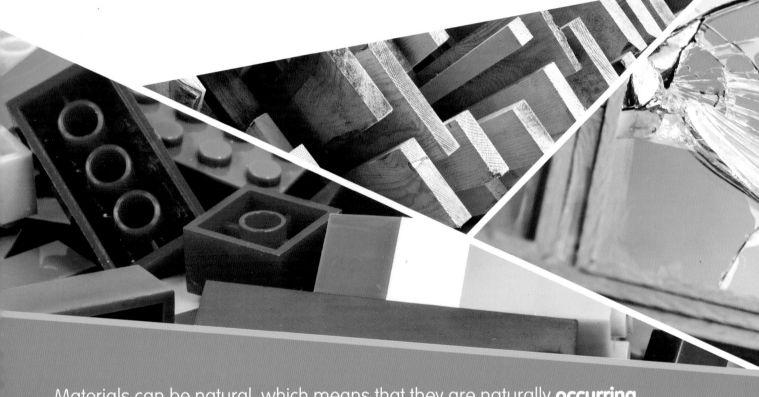

Materials can be natural, which means that they are naturally **occurring** on planet Earth. Materials can also be man-made, which means that they have been made or caused by humans.

PLASTIC IS A MAN-MADE MATERIAL.

WOOD IS A NATURAL MATERIAL.

PROPERTIES OF MATERIALS

Every material has its own properties that make it useful for particular jobs. A material could be:

- Transparent (see-through) or opaque (not see-through)
- Heavy or light
- Strong or weak
- Flexible or rigid
- Absorbent or waterproof

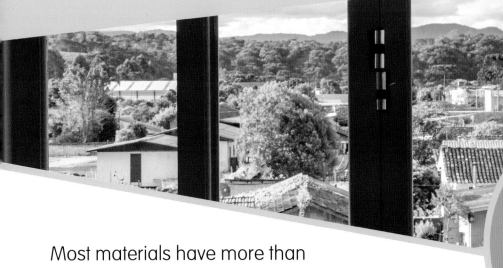

GLASS IS TRANSPARENT.

All materials are either a solid, a liquid or a gas. Some materials, such as water, can change from a liquid to a solid if cooled or to a gas if heated.

Most materials have more than one property. Some types of wood, such as oak, is extremely strong and is used to make furniture. Balsa wood is used to make model aeroplanes because it is light and flexible.

WOODEN TABLE

MODEL AEROPLANE

WOOD

Wood is a hard, **fibrous** material that we get from the trunks and branches of trees. Wood is a naturally occurring material and is one of the most useful and **versatile** on planet Earth. We use wood to make hundreds of different things including tables, chairs and even houses. Other materials which are softer and more **flexible**, such as cardboard and paper, are also made from wood. Tree farms around the world are always planting and growing large numbers of trees that will eventually be cut down and used to make many everyday objects.

Did you know?

When a tree is cut down, the number of rings you can see on the wood inside the trunk tells you how many years old the tree is!

WOOD IN WATER

Wood can act like a sponge, **absorbing** water and swelling in damp conditions. When wood is exposed to water, however, it might begin to **decay** or rot. When this happens, the wood is said to be going rotten. Decay usually makes the wood darker than its natural colour, feel soft and spongy and makes it weak and easy to break.

Wood can be sprayed or painted to protect it from water to stop it from decaying.

WOOD IN HEAT

Wood that is dry can be burnt by fire to produce light and heat. The burning wood will begin to **decompose** and smoke will be produced. As it burns, the rest of the wood forms char, which is made of an element called carbon and ash. This is the white powder-like substance that is left behind after a fire has gone out.

IN ORDER TO START A FIRE, THERE MUST BE HEAT, OXYGEN AND FUEL.

HEAT

Kindling is often used to start a fire because it burns easily.

OXYGEN

FUEL

This symbol means that a material can be recycled.

RECYCLING WOOD

Wood can be recycled, which means it can be used again and again. It is important that we recycle as many natural materials as possible so that we do not continue to take them from the environment. Paper can be recycled if it is taken to a recycling plant. The paper is washed with a type of soap to remove any ink, staples or glue. After being washed, the paper is rolled out into thin sheets and, once it has dried, it can be used again.

WE RECYCLE WOOD SO THAT FEWER TREES NEED TO BE CUT DOWN. WE NEED TREES BECAUSE THEY PROVIDE US WITH OXYGEN THAT WE NEED TO BREATHE TO STAY ALIVE.

PLASTIC

Plastic is a man-made material that is extremely versatile. When plastic is made, it is moulded into the shape of the object required. Once the plastic has set, it cannot be changed unless it is **exposed** to heat in order to make it melt. Plastic can be extremely strong and rigid or light and flexible. Strong plastic can be used to make lunch boxes. The light, thin bags that we use to carry our shopping are also made out of plastic.

Have a look around your classroom. What can you see that might be made out of plastic?

PLASTIC IN WATER

Unlike some other materials, plastic is not damaged when it comes into contact with liquids. The liquid stays on the surface of the plastic and can be easily wiped away. This is because plastic is waterproof. Chairs and tables in gardens are often made out of plastic because they can be left outside without becoming damaged by bad weather.

SOME UMBRELLAS ARE MADE OUT OF PLASTIC SO THAT THEY STOP RAIN FROM FALLING ON US AND MAKING US WET.

PLASTIC IN HEAT

When plastic is heated to a very high temperature, it will melt. When a plastic object has been melted it can be **recast** into a different shape. Once the plastic cools, it is set in the new shape and cannot be changed unless it is melted again. Plastic drinks bottles can be melted down and recast as tables or chairs. It is important that we recycle as many plastic items as possible so that they can be reused.

Be careful!
When plastic melts, it releases gases that can be dangerous if we breathe them in.

TOYS

Plastic is used to make many different toys and games because it is light, but also strong and **durable**. Buckets and spades are often made out of plastic. They are light so they can be carried easily but are strong enough to hold the heavy sand. If they get wet, the water can be wiped away!

Do you have any toys or games that are made out of plastic?

SOME HAND-HELD GAME CONSOLES ARE MADE OUT OF PLASTIC. THEY ARE LIGHT SO YOU CAN HOLD THEM BUT STRONG SO THEY CANNOT BE EASILY BROKEN.

METAL

Metal is a natural material that is found in rocks. There are many different types of metal and each has its own properties that make it useful for particular jobs, for example steel and iron are extremely strong and are often used to make buildings and bridges. Aluminium is a type of metal that is used to make drinks cans. It is a very light metal and one that can easily be bent or reshaped by hand.

Which of these metals can you identify?

METAL IN WATER

When metals that contain iron are exposed to oxygen and **moisture**, they can go rusty. When a metal has gone rusty, it feels rough and flaky and can look red or orange in colour. Metal can be sprayed or painted to protect it so it does not go rusty. Only metals that contain iron will rust, but other metals also **corrode** in similar ways.

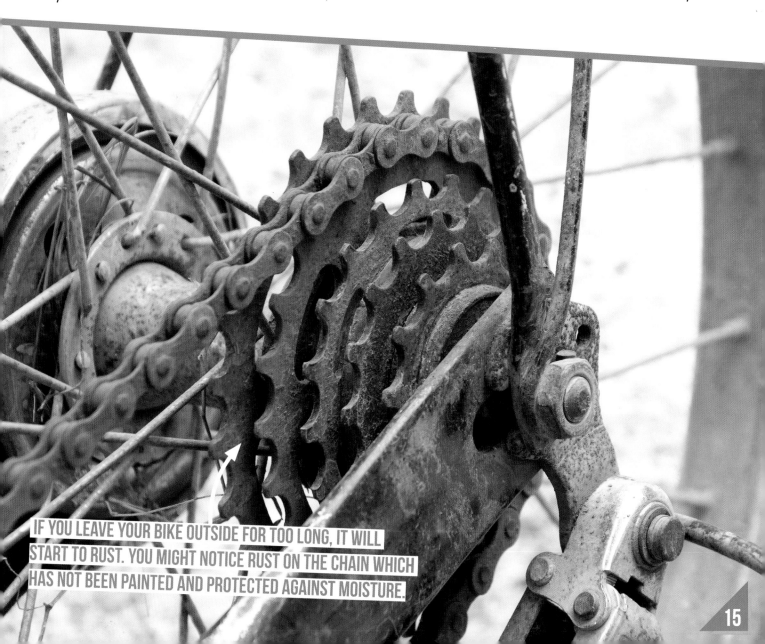

IF YOU LEAVE YOUR BIKE OUTSIDE FOR TOO LONG, IT WILL START TO RUST. YOU MIGHT NOTICE RUST ON THE CHAIN WHICH HAS NOT BEEN PAINTED AND PROTECTED AGAINST MOISTURE.

MAGNETIC METAL

Some types of metal are magnetic. When a magnet is placed near to a magnetic metal, the magnet attracts the metal towards it. Iron is a type of metal that is magnetic. If you hold a magnet near to something made out of iron, for example paperclips or scissors, the object will be attracted towards the magnet.

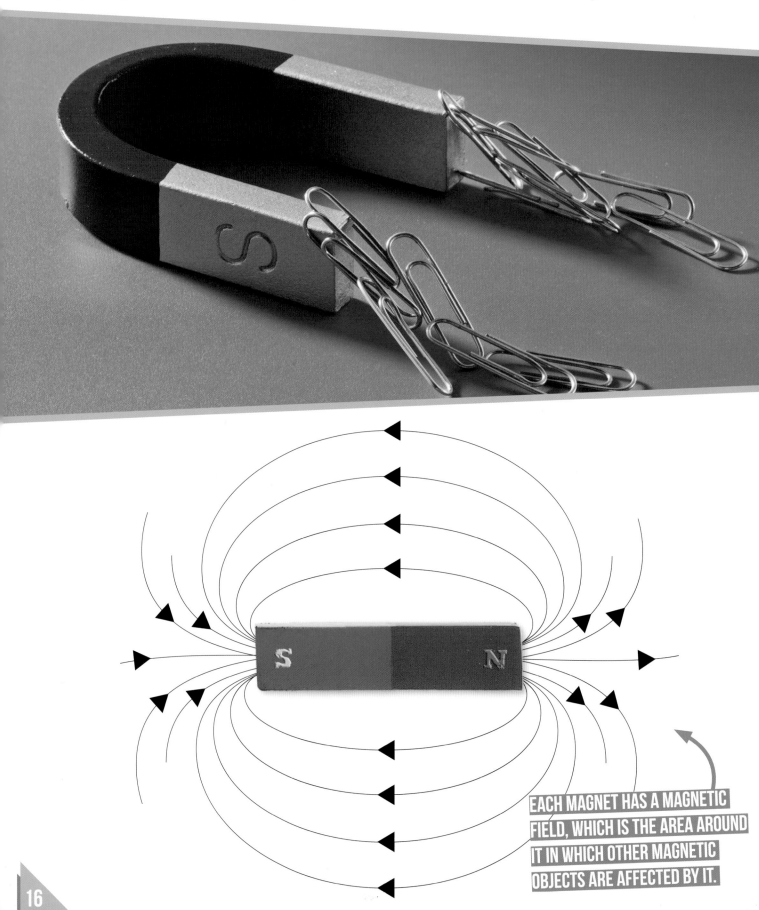

EACH MAGNET HAS A MAGNETIC FIELD, WHICH IS THE AREA AROUND IT IN WHICH OTHER MAGNETIC OBJECTS ARE AFFECTED BY IT.

MUSICAL INSTRUMENTS

Some musical instruments are made out of metal. Metal instruments are often polished to make them look very shiny. Trumpets and trombones are both made of a metal called brass, this is why they belong to the family of brass instruments. The flute is usually made of solid silver. It belongs to the family of woodwind instruments because you have to blow across it in order for it to make a sound.

What other musical instruments can you think of that are made out of metal?

Do you know what type of metal they are made out of?

GLASS

Glass is a solid, man-made material that is made from sand. Glass has many different uses. Glass is transparent and usually feels smooth to touch. It can be strong and hard to break, like the glass used to make windscreens on cars, however, glass can also be weak and fragile. If a glass vase is dropped, it will usually shatter.

BE CAREFUL NOT TO TOUCH ANY BROKEN GLASS. IT CAN BE VERY SHARP AND COULD CUT YOU.

USES OF GLASS

Strong glass is used to make windows in houses and cars because it is durable and transparent. Glass can also be used to make bottles and jars, which can be used for storing food and drink such as jam and milk. Glass can be recycled if we take it to special bottle banks. From there it is taken to a factory to be recycled so we can use it again.

GLASS IN WATER

Glass is waterproof, which means that it will not absorb water. Windows are made from glass because it stops rain water getting into houses or cars. Water will not have an effect on glass and can be wiped away easily. When water falls onto the windscreen of a car, the window wipers can wipe away the water quickly and easily so that we can see where we are going.

GLASS IN HEAT

Glass is made by heating several different materials, the most important of which is sand, at a very high temperature. As they are heated, the different materials turn into liquid glass. Whilst it is a liquid, glass can be blown, poured or moulded to make a range of different shapes. As the glass cools, it becomes solid. The shape that has been made cannot be changed unless it is melted again.

THIS IS HOW GLASS IS BLOWN.

ROCK

Rock is a naturally occurring material that is found all over planet Earth. Rocks are made of minerals and each rock is made up of at least two different types of mineral that are packed together. We use some types of rock in our homes. Granite is often used to make kitchen worktops because it is hard, strong and durable.

LIMESTONE CAN BE USED TO BUILD HOUSES.

MARBLE

MANY PEOPLE LIKE THE APPEARANCE OF MARBLE AND SO IT IS OFTEN USED TO MAKE FLOORS AND STATUES.

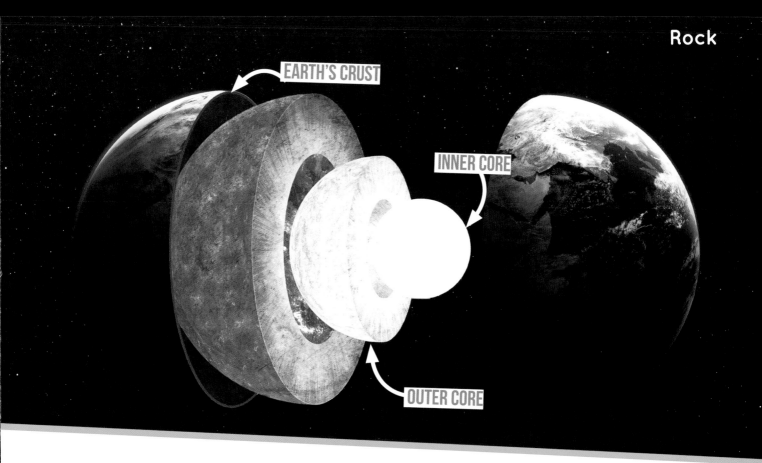

EARTH'S CRUST

INNER CORE

OUTER CORE

ROCK IN HEAT

It takes a temperature of anywhere between 600 and 1,300 degrees Celsius to melt rock. When a rock melts, it changes into a substance called lava. The high temperatures needed to melt rock are mostly only found inside the Earth's **core**. Rocks are pushed downwards as the surface layer of the Earth, called the crust, moves. As the rocks are pushed deeper towards the Earth's core, the temperature gets hotter and hotter, causing the rocks to melt.

TYPES OF ROCK

Rocks are organised into three main groups: igneous, sedimentary and metamorphic. All rocks can be put into one of these three groups based on their properties. Scientists can identify different types of rock by how hard they are and by the way they look. Rocks can be different colours, have layers or holes or they might even be **reflective**.

IGNEOUS ROCK

Igneous rocks are made when hot magma cools. Igneous rocks, such as gabbro, usually have visible crystals inside of them.

GABBRO

SEDIMENTARY ROCK

Rivers and streams carry pieces of rock as they flow and when the water reaches a lake or sea, the rocks are **deposited** at the bottom. While these tiny rocks build up, the weight of the water above pushes them down and squeezes the water out of all the gaps in-between the rocks. Over time, these tiny pieces of rock come together to form larger, sedimentary rocks. This type of rock will usually have a layered appearance.

SEDIMENTARY ROCK (SANDSTONE)

METAMORPHIC ROCK

Metamorphic rocks are formed when rocks are put under very high heat and pressure. Lapis lazuli is a type of metamorphic rock that is often used to make jewellery.

LAPIS LAZULI

WATER

Water is a natural material that is mostly found in seas, rivers, lakes and below the ground. It is a liquid that has no taste or smell and is transparent. Water is an extremely important resource and is essential for life on planet Earth. We use water for many different things, including drinking, cooking and cleaning.

Water can also be used to produce electricity. Water or hydro turbines collect and store energy produced by flowing or falling water. A **generator** then converts this energy into electrical power.

Water covers over 70% of the Earth's surface.

PROPERTIES OF WATER

Water can either be a solid, a liquid or a gas. When water is solid, it is called ice. Ice is extremely cold to touch. Water in a liquid state will take the shape of the space it is given, for example when you pour water into a glass it takes the shape of that glass. When water is a gas it is called steam or water vapour and it can be extremely hot to touch.

ICE

WATER

STEAM

HEATING AND COOLING WATER

When water is colder than 0 degrees Celsius, it freezes and becomes ice. Water that has salt in it, for example sea water, can sometimes only freeze at much colder temperatures. When the weather is cold enough, rain water will freeze as it falls to the ground and when this happens, it is snowing. When water is heated to a temperature of 100 degrees Celsius, it becomes a gas called steam. This process is called evaporation. Steam is made out of tiny droplets of water and it looks like white mist. When the droplets cool, they turn back into liquid. This process is called condensation.

WATER AROUND THE WORLD

Angel Falls in the country of Venezuela is the tallest waterfall in the world. The water drops 807 metres before it hits the ground. The waterfall is around 15 times higher than the famous Niagara Falls found in the countries of Canada and the USA.

ANGEL FALLS

The River Nile in Africa is the longest river in the world; it is 4,160 miles long. Many people live next to the River Nile and use its water for cooking, cleaning and growing crops.

RIVER NILE

FUN FACTS

Most of the Earth's fresh water, which is water that is clean enough for us to drink, is frozen in polar ice caps and glaciers.

Most families use around 330 glass bottles and jars every single year.

The middle of planet Earth, called the core, is made out of iron and nickel, which are both types of metal.

160,000 plastic bags are used around the world every single second.

Some trees that are still living on planet Earth are over 2,000 years old.

The average person uses around 150 litres of water every day.

GLOSSARY

absorbing	to gradually take something in
core	the middle part of something
corrode	when a material is slowly damaged, often by water
decay	to cause something to be gradually damaged
decompose	to decay
deposited	to have left something somewhere
durable	able to last for a long time without becoming damaged
exposed	to have made something able to be seen
fibrous	something that is made of thread-like structures
flexible	able to bend
generator	a machine used to turn energy into electricity
moisture	a liquid in the form of very small drops
occurring	happening
recast	when something is put into a cast, or mould, and as a result is made into a different shape
reflective	something that bounces back the light that shines on it, so it can be easily seen
substances	things with physical characteristics
versatile	able to be used for many different purposes

INDEX

absorbent 5

absorbing 7, 20

Celsius 23, 28

cleaning 26, 29

condensation 28

cooking 26, 29

crops 29

Earth 4, 6, 22–23, 26, 30

evaporation 28

factories 19

flexible 5–6, 10

games 13

gases 5, 12, 27–28

heat 5, 8, 10, 12, 21, 23, 25, 28

heavy 5, 13

houses 6, 19–20, 22

ice 27–28

igneous rock 24

iron 14–16, 30

instruments 17

jewellery 25

lava 23

light 5, 8, 10, 13–14

liquids 5, 11, 21, 26–28

litres 30

magma 24

magnetic 16

man–made 4, 10, 18

melts 10, 12, 21, 23

metals 14–17, 30

metamorphic rock 24–25

mist 28

natural 4, 6–7, 9, 14, 22, 26

oxygen 8–9, 15

paper 6, 9

plastic 4, 10–13, 30

recycled 9, 12, 19

rivers 25–26, 29

rocks 14, 22–25,

rotten 7

sand 13, 18, 21, 25

sedimentary rock 24–25,

solids 5, 17–18, 21, 27

steel 14

strong 5, 10, 13–14, 18–19, 22

temperatures 12, 21, 23, 28

toys 13

transparent 5, 18–19, 26

trees 6, 9, 30

water 5, 7, 11, 13, 15, 20, 25–30

waterproof 5, 11, 20

weather 11, 28

wood 4–9

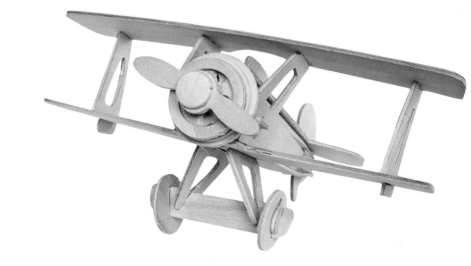